# gratitude

---

**'GRA-TA-TÜD**
NOUN

THE QUALITY OF BEING THANKFUL;
READINESS TO SHOW APPRECIATION FOR
AND TO RETURN KINDNESS.

---

# INTRODUCTION

## THIS BEAUTIFUL JOURNAL IS FILLED WITH SIMPLE IDEAS OF THINGS YOU CAN BE GRATEFUL FOR AND THAT CAN REALLY CHANGE YOUR LIFE FOR THE BETTER.

Nearly always in life, it is the simple things, and sometimes even the things we complain about, that are actually the ones that give us true joy. When we are in a constant state of rushing, it is hard to see the wonderful gifts that surround us, so we urge you to take a moment, grab a cup of tea, and flip through these pages.

## WHAT EXACTLY IS GRATITUDE?

Gratitude is simply showing appreciation or being thankful. When we are busy, in the rush of daily life, it can be the last thing we think of. Do you wake each morning and give thanks for another day of life? Probably not, but well done if you do. We tend to rush into each day, alarms going off, places to be, things to do. Wouldn't it be a wonderful way to start the day, though? Just taking a moment to realize the gift of another day.

## GRATITUDE IS YOUR SUPERPOWER.

Gratitude is amazing. It gives us the ability to flip negatives into positives. Even in the darkest situations, if we give it time, we can see things we can be grateful for. Lessons to be learned, love given, acts of kindness from others, building character, and so on. The secret is practicing. Just like a muscle, the more you use it, the stronger it becomes. Using gratitude helps you strengthen your brain to seek out the good, and in turn, raise your levels of happiness. You don't need to change your world to be happier; you simply need to change your mind, and gratitude helps you do just that.

When practicing gratitude, adding emotions gives it real power. By simply adding "because" to anything you are grateful for will make you think about why. Why are you grateful for your pet? Because they give you unconditional love. How does that make you feel? Truly loved, happy . . . GRATEFUL! Simply saying, "I'm grateful for my dog," just isn't the same. It's only half the story and it doesn't unleash the superpower of gratitude.

Starting out, it can be hard to think of things to be grateful for and why, so the contents of this book are simple reminders of some of the wonderful things that we can be grateful for—if we simply stop and notice. When we remind ourselves that these are important things, it makes life's choices a lot simpler.

*Finding Gratitude: A Journal* is divided into four sections—The Natural World, Everyday Comforts, Human Connections, and My Mind, Body, and Spirit—with gratitude prompts to get you writing. While not every page may apply to you and your life, we hope that most of them will. There's no right or wrong way to use this journal. The point is to get you thinking and practicing gratitude.

**SEE THE GOOD IN THE WORLD, BECAUSE THERE REALLY IS SO MUCH OF IT. SEE THE WONDER IN THE WORLD, BECAUSE WE ARE SURROUNDED BY IT.**

TRUE MIRACLES ARE

FOUND IN THE

*natural world.*

# the
# natural
# world

# NATURE

Nature is such a constant source of joy in my life and reminds me how resilient life truly is, with its beauty and power. It makes me feel connected in an often-disconnected world and resets me and brings me back into balance. I always feel like I belong in nature and it never fails to welcome and reward me. I am grateful that nature is a wonderful teacher that has so much wisdom to offer, if I stop and listen. Nature makes me feel at peace and reduces my stress levels. It grounds me to the Earth and is where I go to find true meaning and connection to something greater than myself. I feel through nature that it connects me to my ancestors and reminds me how everything is connected and important. Nature represents change as a constant and necessary process and teaches me about diversity and how beauty is represented in so many different forms. It allows me to slow down and just "be." It is so fascinating and totally captivates and inspires me. I am truly thankful for nature and how astonishingly beautiful and amazing it is. It makes me feel happy and at peace with the world by just being at one with it.

*I am grateful for nature because . . .*

# STARS

Stars have inspired so many people to search for meaning. They fill me with a sense of wonder and let me know that the universe is vast and limitless. I am really blown away with the sheer size of it all and the stars remind me how small I am, and in turn, how much smaller my problems are. The stars shine bright like beautiful diamonds in the sky and I love making wishes on them. So many of our festivals and traditions are based on the stars and people have studied them forever and learned many things from them. When I look at the stars, they remind me of loved ones who are no longer with us. There is something truly breathtaking looking up into the night sky filled with wonderful stars.

*I am grateful for stars because . . .*

# RAIN

I love the sound of raindrops on the roof; It relaxes me when I am inside, warm and dry. The sound of rain soothes me to sleep and gives me a perfect reason to stay in bed or relax inside, reading a book or watching movies. Rain waters the Earth and fills up my water tank so that I have drinking water, and for that I am truly grateful. Rain is such a delight to see after a long, hot summer. It fills up our rivers and lakes and nourishes the plants, so they can grow. I love the smell of rain and it is so refreshing when I am hot. Sometimes, it is wonderful to stand in rain, just as a child would, and to dance and play in it.

*I am grateful for rain because . . .*

I AM GRATEFUL FOR

# ANIMALS

There are many different animals on the planet and they each can teach important lessons about life. They make me laugh and are super cute. They can make wonderful companions and make me feel valued and important when I care for them. They are nonjudgmental and provide me with unconditional love. Animals aren't complicated, and they bring so much joy to the world. They are magnificent and majestic and spark my imagination. Animals are part of the circle of life and make me happy to be surrounded by them. The world just wouldn't be the same without them, so I am thankful that we have so many kinds of animals on Earth.

# I am grateful for animals because . . .

# RAINBOWS

Rainbows are such a wonderful sight to see.
They draw you into the present moment
and often can be a symbol or sign from the
universe. They give hope that something
great is waiting at the end of a journey.
They are a sign that there is always hope
for a brighter day. Rainbows mean the sun
is shining through the rain and they feel so
magical. Rainbows can represent luck and
make me look for the pot of gold in my
own journey through life. Rainbows always
put a smile on my face because they are so
beautiful in the sky.

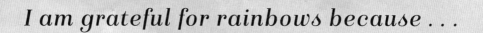

*I am grateful for rainbows because . . .*

I AM GRATEFUL FOR

# THE OCEAN

Whenever I swim in the ocean, it feels
like I am washing away my worries. I am
so grateful to walk barefoot on the sand,
and simply standing next to the ocean
grounds me to the Earth. The salty sea air is
so refreshing; it blows away any stress and
helps connect me to nature. The ocean is
so powerful and vast, filled with some of
the most amazing creatures. It has such an
array of life and many places are yet to be
explored. As I listen to the waves crashing,
I feel so grateful to be alive and to be in
this moment. The sound of the ocean is so
relaxing, and it restores me. I am grateful for
the abundance that the ocean holds, which
provides food and is a place I can come and
enjoy with family and friends. The ocean
helps me to be present in the moment; it
replenishes and rejuvenates my soul and
makes me feel so alive.

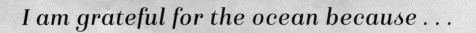

*I am grateful for the ocean because . . .*

## I AM GRATEFUL FOR

# THE SUN

Sunlight is essential for all life on the planet. The sun never fails to make an appearance and is a beacon of light that allows me to see. Without the sun, the moon wouldn't shine. The sun warms the oceans and the lakes. It puts on amazing displays at sunrise and sunset each day for me to witness and provides me with much-needed vitamin D. I am always very grateful when the sun warms my skin and the Earth. It helps all the plants grow and, in turn, they nourish me. The sun provides renewable and clean energy for the planet and helps me power my home. I am so grateful for the sun because we need it to survive.

*I am grateful for the sun because . . .*

# SUNRISES

When the sun rises, it means it is a new day, a new chance. It takes place every day, whether it is witnessed or not. I am so grateful when I make the effort to get up and watch it, as it is ALWAYS worth it. A sunrise is wondrous and signals new beginnings and hope for the future. Every day it is unique and always changing. It is as if the universe is putting on a show just for me. It really is a magical time of the day, when the animals are just waking up and I get to enjoy the birds singing. No matter where in the world you are, or who you are, you get to witness it for free. It is signaling to my part of the world to awaken. It happens quite quickly, so I am grateful for the times I get to view it as it ignites my soul with energy.

*I am grateful for sunrises because . . .*

# SUNSETS

I made it through another day and that makes me feel happy. Watching the sun setting is such a gorgeous way to end the day and it is so strikingly beautiful. It allows me to be more mindful because I know that the sun is rising somewhere else on the planet for others to enjoy. I am grateful for sunsets as it signals a time to rest and is a symbol for endings, which gives way to new beginnings. Sunsets reminds me of the wonder of how the solar system works, and that the Earth is spinning on its axis as it moves around the sun—this really is quite amazing when you stop and think about it. The sunrays are buttery and lovely at the end of day. When the sun sets, the sky changes quickly with different colors and shades, like a changing work of art. Every sunset is different and mesmerizing, and I am thankful for every single one that I get to witness.

# I am grateful for sunsets because . . .

I AM GRATEFUL FOR

# TREES

Trees are strong and magnificent, and they come in all shapes and sizes. I am grateful for the oxygen they provide me, so I can breathe easily. They also supply me with building materials and fuel to keep my family and me warm. Trees teach me about establishing foundations to grow strong and resilient, and to never give up. They provide me with shelter and shade as well as an array of delicious fruits and nuts. Trees are a fabulous source of creativity, displaying their different shapes, sizes, and diversity. They are gorgeous, especially in spring when they start blossoming, and then again in autumn, when the leaves change colors. I am thankful to the trees for cleaning the air that humans pollute. I really enjoying hugging them and appreciate the quality of life they give me. They are so much a part of the life cycle on Earth in the present moment, as well as providing a connection to the past. I am grateful for trees and the sense of peace they create within me. They reduce my stress, making me feel calm and at one with nature.

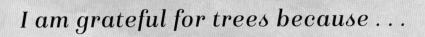

*I am grateful for trees because . . .*

**I AM GRATEFUL FOR**

# FLOWERS

Flowers are colorful and lift my spirits almost instantly when I look at them. I am grateful for the pollen they provide for the bees and their medicinal properties, which can help relieve all sorts of ailments. Flowers make my home look welcoming when others come to visit and make such a wonderful gift for others. Sometimes when I don't have the words, flowers can show I care. I know that whenever I receive flowers, I feel loved and appreciated. Flowers signal that warmer weather is coming and help get me out into the garden. I love that they attract wonderful creatures to the garden, and they just make me feel happy. Flowers are a symbol of so many things and hold valuable lessons about life. They are all so unique and beautiful in their own way. They can turn into delicious fruits, vegetables, and nuts, which nourish my body. Flowers make the world look exquisite and help to decrease air pollution. They often spark creativity and romance. I am grateful for the gorgeous fragrance that so many flowers have. Flowers really are beautiful.

*I am grateful for flowers because . . .*

**I AM GRATEFUL FOR**

# WINTER

Winter allows me time to do less. It means long nights in front of the fire and cozy blankets to snuggle into. I love coming inside from the cold and enjoying hot soups and hearty meals. It means more cuddles to keep warm and curling up to read a book by the fire, and it is a great time for rest and renewal. Winter means snowboarding and skiing trips, followed by hot chocolate. I love looking out at the snow-covered mountains and enjoying winter festivals. It is a time for lovely big meals with family and making snow angels. It is a time for slippers and dressing gowns. In winter nature teaches me to slow down. The trees are bare, showing me that vulnerability is part of a process. The air is so crisp, and I love seeing my breath when I exhale.

*I am grateful for winter because . . .*

# SPRING

Springtime reminds me that I can start again. The new blossoms that adorn the trees are so beautiful. The weather starts to slowly warm up after the cold months and everything bursts into life. There is a sense of hope in the air. Birds start singing again. Spring is a time of wanting to get outside again. In the animal kingdom, babies are born. Nature wakes up after a long sleep and signals for me to do the same. It is a great time to spring-clean my home so it feels fresh and decluttered. I am so grateful for all the delicious fruits and vegetables that start coming into season again and my garden bursts into life. Beautiful flowers appear everywhere, and I can open all the doors and windows again to let in the crisp, fresh air. I love not having to wear so many layers of clothing and feeling a bit of warmth in the days again.

*I am grateful for spring because . . .*

## I AM GRATEFUL FOR

# SUMMER

Summer means I get to be outside and enjoy nature more often. It means lots of swimming in oceans, lakes, and rivers. I can wear sandals instead of shoes, and I get to enjoy the warm sunshine on my skin. I love summer because I can roast marshmallows over bonfires and enjoy the sound of the ice-cream truck and the treats it brings. I feel so happy to wake up on a beautiful summer's day. Everyone seems to be happier. There are summer holidays with friends and family where we can eat dinner outside and enjoy the long, warm evenings. Summer is a time of concerts and festivals and of days spent boating and fishing. I am grateful for a lovely, cool cocktail or smoothie that goes along with my lighter summer meals of salads and fruit. Summer is the smell of sunscreen and a time of year I look forward to.

# I am grateful for summer because . . .

# AUTUMN

Autumn is my favorite time of the year.
With all the beautiful colors of the trees, it
signals that a change is ahead. The festivals
celebrate the changing of the season and
it means eating more comfort foods like
soups. After a long, hot summer, it starts to
cool slightly, which means chilly mornings
with warm afternoons. Delicious autumn
fruits and vegetables can be enjoyed, and
the garden becomes easier to manage.
In autumn I get the best of summer and
winter, all in one day. Mother Nature
reminds us to start slowing down. The
beautiful crisp air is refreshing and makes
me feel alive. There are gorgeous leaves
everywhere in yellows, oranges, and browns
that are so much fun to play in. Sleeping
becomes more enjoyable with the cooler
nights. Autumn signals a time to shed the
old and allows us to look forward to a time
of rest.

*I am grateful for autumn because . . .*

*Beauty is*

EVERYWHERE;
OPEN YOUR EYES
AND SEE IT.

*everyday comforts*

## I AM GRATEFUL FOR

# WATER

Water is refreshing and a source of life. It hydrates my body and keeps me alive. It helps me to stay clean as well as cleaning my home and everything in it. Water is peaceful and calms me by just looking and listening to it. I am amazed at how essential it is for all aspects of life on Earth. Water washes away my worries, making me feel relaxed and rejuvenated. It nourishes the Earth and everything living on it. I can swim and play in it. It replenishes my body and soul, and I am grateful for every drop.

# I am grateful for water because . . .

## I AM GRATEFUL FOR

# FOOD

Food gives me such pleasure. I really enjoy eating and cooking for myself and others. Food gives me energy to do all the things I need to do. It nourishes my body, and there are so many different varieties and flavors to try. We cannot live without it, so I am thankful to have easy access to a range of foods. It can look stunning and colorful and bring people together. I am thankful for every meal I get to enjoy, especially if someone else cooks for me.

# I am grateful for food because . . .

I AM GRATEFUL FOR

# FIRE

Fire mesmerizes me. Warmth is one of the
basics I need to stay alive and a fire makes
my home toasty. I love sitting around it
with family and friends, as it is a great
way to connect. An outside fire is great for
gatherings and to toast marshmallows over.
Fire allows me to cook, and it makes me feel
protected and safe. Sitting in front of a fire
helps me to feel calm and relaxed.

# I am grateful for fire because . . .

# MY HOME

My home is my favorite place to be in the world. It is a place full of the people I love and a place where I feel safe and secure. It has all the things I love in it and provides my family with shelter from the elements. It is where family and friends congregate, and we have lots of fun times and create memories together. Home is a place where I can unwind and relax. When I go away, I am always happy when I return home. Home is a place my children can always come back to and we always have room for other people to stay. My home is warm and cozy and in a beautiful spot in the world. It is the one place where I can be my authentic self. My home is my little piece of paradise.

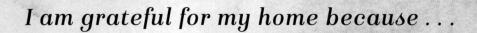

*I am grateful for my home because . . .*

I AM GRATEFUL FOR

# WORK

Working allows me to make money and provide for myself and my family. It allows me to be part of society and gives me a sense of worth. Working means I can use the money I make to spend on the things that I need and love. It also allows me to meet interesting, new people and challenges me to be innovative and learn new things. I can also work with others toward a common goal and it gives me an outlet for my creativity. Through my work, I can help others and I have made some great friends too.

# I am grateful for work because . . .

# MY BED

My bed is my sanctuary. It is warm and cozy, and I look forward to climbing into it. It is where I get to lay my head for much-needed sleep, the place where I can rest and recover. It is the place where I can snuggle up to the one I love. My pets like to keep me company there. It is where my children come to cuddle with me when they are scared at night. I am very grateful to have a bed of my own and it is one of my favorite places to be. I absolutely love the feeling of getting into bed after a long day.

# I am grateful for my bed because . . .

**I AM GRATEFUL FOR**

# SHOWERS

Showers help me wake up in the morning. When I feel chilled, a hot shower warms me up. It means I can easily clean myself, while helping me relax and unwind. After having a shower, I feel clean and smell divine. A shower relieves aches and pains and is my alone and quiet time. A hot shower washes away the stresses of the day. I am very lucky to even have a shower and running water. It is a simple joy in life that I am very grateful to be able to enjoy.

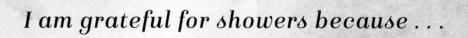

*I am grateful for showers because . . .*

I AM GRATEFUL FOR

# BATHS

Baths help me to relax. Hopping into a bath is such a relief when I have aches and pains, relaxing my muscles. I can unwind and release the stresses of the day. I enjoy adding in some Epsom salts help to detox my body. It is a sancturary where I get some quiet time, a time for self-care. It helps to heal my body and is a great way to clean myself. My children love a bubble bath as much as I do. A bath is one of the best places to read a book. It is a treat to add in special oils and flowers and afford myself some "me" time. A bath feels like a little bit of luxury that I am grateful to have time for.

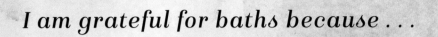

# I am grateful for baths because . . .

**I AM GRATEFUL FOR**

# CLOTHING

Clothing is a way for me to express myself and at the same time keeps me covered. It keeps me warm and dry and protects me from the elements. Clothing allows me to play dress up or transport me to another time. It protects me from scratches if I were to slip or fall and makes me feel comfortable. I love getting dressed up in beautiful clothing as well as designing and making my own clothes. Clothes are a basic need that I am grateful to be able to have so many to choose from.

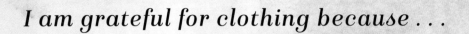

*I am grateful for clothing because . . .*

I AM GRATEFUL FOR

# THE INTERNET

The internet gives me a voice. It can create movements for positive change around the world, as well as enabling me to access people who can help me if I need it. It has helped many people fulfill their dreams, reunited family and friends who have been separated, and provided me with answers to my questions in an instant. The internet allows me to work from home and anywhere else in the world that I may want to. I have made some awesome friends online who have become real-life friends. The internet connects me to people I might never have met and entertains me with all the movies, games, and media available through it. It allows me to be creative and innovative and learn new things. The internet has connected the world.

# I am grateful for the internet because . . .

**I AM GRATEFUL FOR**

# ART

Art comes in all sorts of mediums. It represents someone's creativity. It often imitates nature and can equally be seen in nature. Art is a way to communicate when words cannot. It allows boundaries to be broken, exploring new ways of expressing ourselves. It allows me to tap into all my senses and can emotionally touch my soul. It can tell a story that can connect people and be a path of self-discovery. Art is therapeutic and brings me so much joy. It enriches my life and I couldn't imagine living without it. Art can be confrontational and address real issues. Art makes my soul sing.

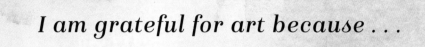

*I am grateful for art because . . .*

# MUSIC

Music stirs up memories and takes me back to another time. It makes me feel warm, alive, and happy. It gets me up and moving and motivates me. Music lifts my mood and makes me feel invigorated. I use it to help me get through mundane chores. It touches my soul and makes me feel connected to something more. Music can be cathartic and helps me heal. It can relax me and means I can hear. It makes me feel like I am connecting to an energy source. It connects me to my emotions like nothing else. Music brings people together.

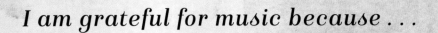

# I am grateful for music because . . .

# BOOKS

Books allow me to learn new things. I can have an adventure without ever going anywhere. They help me expand my mind and gain new skills. I love the feel of a book, the smell and the paper. They can transport me to another time or place and can help me understand new ways of thinking or doing things. Books help me to unwind and de-stress. They help me to escape my worries and can also help me to fall asleep at night. They are beautiful and can spark my imagination. They can make me laugh or cry or both. Books are better than movies and I get to meet the most amazing characters and creatures. They give me something to dream about. Books allow me to tell my story. They are magical and fantastical. Books are my happy place.

# I am grateful for books because . . .

*Little acts*

OF KINDNESS

TO OTHERS

FEED YOUR SOUL.

# human
# connections

**I AM GRATEFUL FOR**

# MY FAMILY

My family always there for me when I need
them the most. They provide me with
unconditional love and accept me for who
I am, faults and all. They give me a sense of
belonging and they can be honest and tell
me things that others might not. They give me
encouragement to follow my dreams. They are
there when I'm at my best and my worst. Even
if we don't always agree, we still love each
other, and they teach me to be accepting of
differences. My family is always there to lend
a helping hand and we can depend on each
other in times of need. Family is where my
heart is, and they mean everything to me.
We have so many laughs together and can
reminisce about old times together. They bring
me so much happiness and support when
times are tough. We are always learning and
growing together. Everything I do is for them
and they are my everrything.

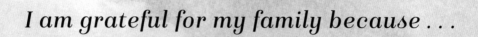

*I am grateful for my family because . . .*

I AM GRATEFUL FOR

# MY MOTHER

My mother loves me like no one else. She can be totally honest with me and has so much wisdom to offer. I am so grateful for all the time she spent caring for me—all the meals she cooked, all the lunches she made, and all the piles of laundry she washed, dried, folded, and put away. She cared for me when I was sick and had lots of sleepless nights because of me. My mother taught me manners and how to be kind to others. She has pushed me to be the best person I can be. She showed me how to be determined and to work hard for the things I want in life. She is always the rock for the family and the one who keeps everyone together. She is a great role model and knows when I need help, sometimes even before I do. She believes in me and is proud of me. I am grateful for all the hugs she gave me when I needed them and for being the person that has my best interests at heart. She makes me laugh and is just awesome. She loves me unconditionally and I love her for all that she has done and will continue to do for me.

# I am grateful for my mother because . . .

I AM GRATEFUL FOR

# MY FATHER

My father loves me and will always love me.
He has worked hard to provide for me and
taught me not to make excuses and to
work hard for what I want. He is kind and
gentle, but at the same time, he protects
me and makes me feel safe. He is always
proud of me and I am grateful for all the
wisdom he shares with me. He is hilarious
and always makes me laugh. He is strict and
that helped shape me into the person I am
today. Beneath his grumpy exterior is a soft
center and he gives the best hugs that make
everything okay again. My father is always
there for me and is someone I can be open
and honest with. I am grateful for all the
time I get with my father.

# I am grateful for my father because . . .

I AM GRATEFUL FOR

# MY SIBLINGS

My siblings inspire me. They understand me like no one else can. They keep me in check and always have my back. My siblings are always there for me when I need them. They are there through good times and bad. I love being with my siblings. They have taught me many lessons, such as how to share and how to be compassionate. I can be totally honest with them and we can laugh about anything and everything together. I can call them any time of the day and night. We can forgive each other even after the worst disagreements. I love them, and they love me.

*I am grateful for my siblings because . . .*

# MY PARTNER

My partner and I are a great team. We work together to make the best life we can. He loves me just the way I am. She supports me unconditionally in the decisions I make, and she is my best friend. He always puts me first, and we are there for each other through thick or thin. She makes me laugh and is my biggest cheerleader. He always encourages me to do my best and to follow my dreams. She makes me feel beautiful and worthy. He sees me at my worst and still loves me. We have so much fun together and she gives me the best hugs when I am sad. He helps me to be a better person and he is loving and kind to me. She gives me the best advice and is my sounding board. He is someone I can confide in and is always there to listen to me. I am so grateful to share my life with her.

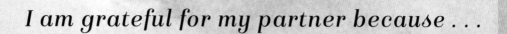

*I am grateful for my partner because . . .*

**I AM GRATEFUL FOR**

# MY PETS

My life just wouldn't be the same without my pets in it. They give amazing cuddles and love me unconditionally. That joy they show when they see me makes me feel so loved and special; it really makes my heart sing and gives me so much joy. They know when I am not feeling well and are there to comfort me. Pets teach us many lessons. They teach us to be responsible, gentle, and caring. They teach us to be compassionate and to live in the moment. My pets are the best companions. They are my reason to get up and out and about. They love me without judgment and accept me for who I am. They help me through rough day. Just petting them, I can feel stress melt away. My pets enrich my life on so many levels and are part of my family.

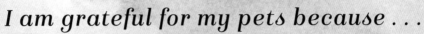

*I am grateful for my pets because . . .*

I AM GRATEFUL FOR

# MY FRIENDS

Friends are there to help me celebrate my successes and are also there when life gets tough. I can talk to them about life and they help me work through challenges. My friends help me calm down when I get upset and often give me a different perspective on things. They motivate me and give me some amazing advice. I couldn't imagine life without them. My friends and I don't have to talk all the time; we know that life can get in the way and that is okay. We have the best times together, filled with fun and laughter. They make my life better and provide me with real-life connections that I need. They are my tribe, the family that I got to handpick. We can make fun of each other and that is okay too. We don't always have to talk or entertain each other, and they allow me to vent when I need to. Life is better with my friends in it.

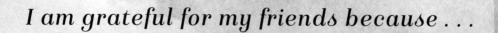

*I am grateful for my friends because . . .*

I AM GRATEFUL FOR

# MY COMMUNITY

My community is very important to me because they support me when times are tough. We all help each other and everyone is familiar with each other. It is nice to know that there are people there for me if I need them. I feel like I belong to something bigger than just me. My community stops me from feeling alone in the world. They make me feel connected and whole. They have helped shape me into the person I have become today, and they encourage me to be the best version of me. It is like having my very own cheerleading squad and I know I can count on them.

*I am grateful for my community because . . .*

## I AM GRATEFUL FOR

# SENIORS

Seniors are our connection to our ancestors.
They have amazing stories to share and have
often sacrificed so much for us. I am grateful
to have spent time with many wonderful
seniors, as they helped to shape me into
the person I am today. They fought for
inequalities that make my life easier today.
They are so inspiring with the great things
they achieved, and they form an important
part of society. The seniors in my life help
me with my children and have such a
positive influence on me. They remind me
to appreciate the simple things in life and
show me where I will be one day and how I
might like to be treated. I am so grateful they
enrich my life with their wisdom and humor.

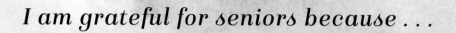

# I am grateful for seniors because . . .

I AM GRATEFUL FOR

# CHILDREN

Children help me to remember how to
live in the moment. They remind me how
to have fun and believe in magic. They ask
lots of questions and are filled with wonder.
Children teach me to be curious and never
give up. They trust me entirely and love
me, faults and all. They enjoy life's simple
pleasures and I am grateful that they remind
me to do the same. They express their
emotions fully and are completely honest.
Children do things their own way and always
make me laugh with the funny things they
say. They represent the generations before
them and are little balls of fun. They teach
me to be resilient and forgiving.

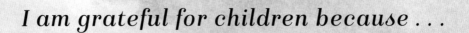

*I am grateful for children because . . .*

**I AM GRATEFUL FOR**

# TRADITIONS

The traditions I grew up with as a child
provide me with a sense of identity.
They are times to celebrate and give me
something to look forward to. Traditions
teach me about what my ancestors valued
and bind us together over generations.
They build strong relationships and help us
remember great lessons and stories from
long ago. They teach us values and morals
and help create routines in our busy lives.
Traditions create stronger families and
communities, providing real connections
that foster love and belonging. Traditions
create lasting memories.

I am grateful for traditions because . . .

I AM GRATEFUL FOR

# FAMILY MEALS

Family meals allow me to spend quality time
with the ones I love. It is a wonderful feeling
to share a meal with everyone. and connect
and talk about our day—time when we can
listen to each other without distractions.
It is a fabulous place to share important
milestones, while being good for our health.
It also means I am part of a family and it can
be the only time of the day when we are all
together. Family mealtime often ends up
in laughter and is an important ritual in our
home, one that I look forward to each day.

*I am grateful for family meals because . . .*

**I AM GRATEFUL FOR**

# HUGS

Hugs make everything feel better. They heal me and cheer me up when I feel sad. Hugging is a way to communicate love without having to speak. It is sharing a space with another person you care about. Hugs make me feel calm and less anxious and are a great way of showing my appreciation. Hugs can lower my heart rate, strengthen my immune system, and reduce stress. Hugging is such a great way to celebrate with someone and it makes me feel loved and show my love. I am so grateful for all the hugs I get. They give me warm fuzzies inside and make me so happy. I couldn't imagine a life without hugs.

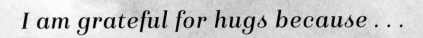

*I am grateful for hugs because . . .*

*Focus on the good*

AND SOON YOU WILL

SEE MORE,

ENJOY MORE,

APPRECIATE MORE.

my mind,
body,
and spirit

I AM GRATEFUL FOR

# MY HEALTH

Being healthy allows me to fully live my life. Everything is better when I feel healthy and it means that my body is functioning well. It means I get to enjoy things completely with nothing holding me back. If I have good health, it means I am looking after myself well, that my body is a temple and it makes me feel amazing. It is important to me to work hard to ensure I am at my optimum, because without our health, life can be a struggle. Being healthy feels good. Health is wealth.

# I am grateful for my health because . . .

**I AM GRATEFUL FOR**

# MY MIND

My mind allows me to wonder and think.
It allows me to recognize and remember
those who I love. It forms my memories for
me as I live my life. It helps me figure out
difficult situations and helps me make good
decisions. My mind allows me to think things
through and learn new things. It means I
can think about others and have empathy.
It operates my body without asking it to and
that is amazing. It allows me to experience
emotions and understand the world through
the information my senses send to it. It helps
make me who I am.

# I am grateful for my mind because . . .

# EMOTIONS

My emotions mean I am alive and human. They allow me to feel and experience the world fully. They can be a great release and allow me to communicate with others. I can express how I feel through them and they help guide me through life. Emotions can unite and connect us. They help me remember things and keep me safe. They provide me with information about what I need and what I really want in life. Emotions are ever-changing, coming and going like waves. Feeling sad some days helps me to appreciate feeling wonderful other days.

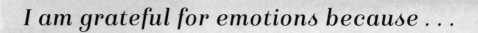

*I am grateful for emotions because . . .*

# MY SENSES

My sight means I can see the world and everything in it. My hearing means I can hear the wonderful sounds like laughter and the waves of the ocean. Touch allows me to feel a warm embrace from someone I love. Taste means I get to enjoy the amazing food the world has to offer. Smell lets me experience a fresh spring day. Even if one of my senses doesn't work, the others will compensate to make my life easier. My senses allow me to fully experience life in the most outstanding ways.

*I am grateful for my senses because . . .*

I AM GRATEFUL FOR

# MY BREATH

My breath allows me to calm myself down and brings me back to the simple things in life that we need to survive. By controlling my breath, it allows me to endure painful experiences and grounds me. It makes me mindfully stop and reset and brings me back to my center to create peace within me. Breathing is the essence of life and is something that I can control that has a positive effect on my health. It floods my body with oxygen so that my cells can renew. Breathing allows me to connect with my body and mind and it helps me to completely relax. Breathing correctly enhances my performance in physical activities and can take me out of fight or flight mode. My breathing means I am alive.

# I am grateful for my breath because . . .

I AM GRATEFUL FOR

# MOVEMENT

Being able to move my body is fun. It keeps
me fit and healthy and allows me to do
so many things. Movement gets my heart
pumping and blood flowing through my
body. It helps to keep my mind healthy and
is a great way to reduce stress. Movement is
a creative outlet for me and makes me feel
alive. Being able to move means my body is
working well and it cleanses me from within.
Movement gives me a way to express myself
and is an outlet for my creativity. Moving
means I am active and allows me to get out
and explore the world as well as accessing
the things I need. Through movement I can
participate in the sports and activities that I
love. Moving is like freeing the spirit within.

# I am grateful for movement because . . .

I AM GRATEFUL FOR

# FAITH

Faith gives meaning to my life. It allows me to
not always have to have all the answers. It gives
me hope, no matter the situation. Faith gives me
the courage to attempt the impossible and the
strength to carry on through the darkest of times.
We are all searching for greater meaning and my
faith provides that for me. It gives me something
to believe in and guides me and gives me purpose.
Everything is easier in life when I have my faith
within me. It allows me to let go of fears and worries,
knowing that things will work out exactly as they
are meant to. I am given signs throughout my life
that strengthen my faith and for that I am grateful.
My faith helps me to be a better person and makes
my soul at peace. It allows me to feel assured that
everything will be okay, and it leads me to true
happiness and abundance. Faith guides me in
everything I do, and it is where I turn to ensure I
am on the right path. My faith is my everything.

*I am grateful for faith because . . .*

# KINDNESS

Kindness from others is a reminder to me to also be kind. It makes me feel special when someone does something kind for me; it helps restore my faith in humanity. Kindness is a beautiful part of being a human. Doing something kind for another for no benefit is truly wonderful. I am grateful for all the kindness offered to me in life and it makes me want to pass it on. Kindness really does foster more kindness. It helps me through life having others be kind and helpful and it brings me so much joy. It is beautiful to witness someone being kind. Kindness really can change the world and is a special kind of magic. When I do something kind for others, I get such a great feeling inside. It boosts my own self-worth and makes me feel good.

*I am grateful for kindness because . . .*

**I AM GRATEFUL FOR**

# SILENCE

Silence allows me time to focus and not be distracted. It makes me feel calm and connected. It allows me to hear the softer sounds from the Earth, like bees buzzing or a river running. Silence means I can just breathe and relax. I crave it and it helps me to think clearly. It is a nice change from the constant noise of a busy life. Silence helps stop the overload of information that I am surrounded with. I am so grateful for the peace that silence creates for me.

*I am grateful for silence because . . .*

**I AM GRATEFUL FOR**

# CREATIVITY

Creativity fires my soul. The most beautiful things can be made with it and it can inspire me in the most unexpected ways. Creativity can be sparked at any moment and gives me renewed energy. Through my creativity, there is no black and white or right and wrong, it drives me to discover answers and truths. I am grateful for all the amazing things that are invented by the creative people in the world. Creativity allows me to break into new territories and see things from a different perspective. It allows me to express myself in any manner of ways and express my individuality. I am grateful for the amazing things that have been produced through my own creativity that enriches my life daily.

# I am grateful for creativity because . . .

I AM GRATEFUL FOR

# INSPIRATION

Inspiration can happen at any given
moment. It propels me forward into
the unknown and I am grateful for the
opportunities that it provides me. Inspiration
excites me and motivates me into action.
It can change the world, and from a small
spark, wonderful things can be created.
Inspiration gives me a relentless drive
to never give up until I reach my goal. It
helps give me vision and awakens me to
new possibilities. I am grateful for inspiring
people as they help me to believe that
anything is possible; they give me the
courage to believe in myself.

*I am grateful for inspiration because . . .*

I AM GRATEFUL FOR

# ACCEPTANCE

Acceptance means I am loved for who I am.
It allows me to grow and challenge myself.
Even though acceptance from others isn't
necessary, it certainly helps me reach my
full potential and feel loved. Acceptance
comes from within. Learning to accept
myself for who I am allows me to live the
life I have always wanted. Accepting myself
for who I am has allowed me to find great
contentment.

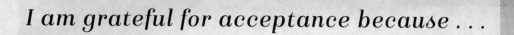

*I am grateful for acceptance because . . .*

## I AM GRATEFUL FOR

# CHALLENGES

Challenges make me feel like I have accomplished
something great when I have worked so hard to
get through them. They force me to think outside
the box and grow and evolve into a better version
of myself. Challenges help me learn to focus on
what is important and make me stronger and
more resilient. I am grateful for the challenges life
has thrown my way, as they let me see what I can
truly achieve. Without them I wouldn't be who I
am today. They keep me on my toes and are the
best way to learn. They force me to look for the
positives in difficult situations and to see there is
always something wonderful in the worst of times.
Often it is after a challenging time that something
wonderful happens, a new stage of growth in
myself or opportunities arise that weren't there
before. I am grateful for the challenges in life, as
they help me to relate better to other people who
have been through similar situations.

*I am grateful for challenges because . . .*

**I AM GRATEFUL FOR**

# LAUGHTER

Laughter fills my body with joy and helps me release stress and tension. I am so grateful for a good laugh, as it makes me feel like everything is okay. It lightens the burdens of worry and stress and helps me look for the good in any situation. It relaxes me and is something that can be shared with others. Laughing feels so good and I am grateful for every laugh I get to enjoy in life. I am grateful for all the amazing comedians that help others laugh and help us see the funny side of life.

*I am grateful for laughter because . . .*

# HAVING FUN

Having fun helps me to feel young again. It ignites my inner child and lifts my spirits. I am grateful for the fun moments in life, as they help me be in the moment. It brings people together, uniting them in enjoyment. It fills my cup and helps me release stress and relax. Having fun makes me more productive and function better. It is important to have fun to balance out all the work I do. Having fun creates energy and sparks my creativity. Joy cannot be suppressed and bubbles out during fun times. It makes me feel so happy and want to have more of it in my life.

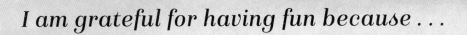

*I am grateful for having fun because . . .*

**I AM GRATEFUL FOR**

# LOVE

Love, more than anything, is what keeps me
going every day. It comes in many forms. It is
what we all crave and is essential in living a
happy life. I am lucky to have lots of it around
me. To be loved and to love are the best
things in the world. Being loved means being
accepted as I am, and that makes me feel
so wonderful. Love helps make the world a
better place. It satisfies my emotional needs,
those that all humans have. It is felt by every
living thing on Earth. Love drives people to
do good and to help one another. It can heal,
and expressing love can make others feel
happier. Love really is the answer and I am
grateful for every bit of love I receive.

# I am grateful for love because . . .

**I AM GRATEFUL FOR**

# ME

I am unique, loving, grateful, and kind. I am constantly evolving and growing. I am funny and can make people laugh. I am creative and resilient. I love helping other people and taking care of those whom I love. I always try to look on the bright side of life and my friends and family can rely on me. I am smart and can figure things out if I need to. I am a wonderful human being who tries my best. I am someone who motivates and inspires others. I learn from my mistakes and I always keep going and keep trying. I am enthusiastic and have great stories to share. I am interested in listening to others. I am an expression of my unique DNA and there is no one else just like me. I am enough!

*I am grateful for me because . . .*

Inspiring | Educating | Creating | Entertaining

Brimming with creative inspiration, how-to projects, and useful information to enrich your everyday life, Quarto Knows is a favorite destination for those pursuing their interests and passions. Visit our site and dig deeper with our books into your area of interest: Quarto Creates, Quarto Cooks, Quarto Homes, Quarto Lives, Quarto Drives, Quarto Explores, Quarto Gifts, or Quarto Kids.

Text © 2019 by Rebekah Lipp and Nicole Perry
Artwork © AwesoME Inc.™

First published in 2019 by Rock Point, an imprint of The Quarto Group,
142 West 36th Street, 4th Floor, New York, NY 10018, USA
T (212) 779-4972 F (212) 779-6058 www.QuartoKnows.com

Rock Point titles are also available at discount for retail, wholesale, promotional and bulk purchase. For details, contact the Special Sales Manager by email at specialsales@quarto.com or by mail at The Quarto Group, Attn: Special Sales Manager, 100 Cummings Center Suite, 265D, Beverly, MA 01915, USA.

ISBN: 978-1-63106-704-4

10 9 8 7 6 5 4 3 2

Editorial Director: Rage Kindelsperger
Creative Director: Laura Drew
Art Director: Cindy Samargia Laun
Designer: Nicole Perry
Managing Editor: Cara Donaldson
Project Editor: Erin Canning
Authors: Rebekah Lipp and Nicole Perry

Printed in China EB032020

This journal provides general information on practicing gratitude. It does not provide any medical information regarding mental or emotional health. The authors and publisher are in no way responsible for any actions or behaviors undertaken by the reader of this book.